30 CROSS-STITCH DESIGNS

Stunning and original cross-stitch projects

SMITHMARK

This edition published in 1996 by
Smithmark Publishers, a division of U.S. Media Holdings Inc.
16 East 32nd Street, New York, NY 10016

Smithmark books are available for bulk purchase and for sales
promotion and for premium use.
For details write or call the Manager of Special Sales, Smithmark
Publishers, 16 East 32nd Street, New York, NY 10016; (212 532-6600)

Produced by
Anness Publishing Limited
1 Boundary Row
London SE1 8HP

Printed and bound in China

10 9 8 7 6 5 4 3 2 1

Contents

INTRODUCTION

D uring the seventeenth century gentlewomen would spend many hours stitching, and the cross stitch subsequently became very popular in sampler work. Later, in the nineteenth century, sewing was a compulsory subject for girls who went to school, and stitching skills were needed to secure jobs as maids and housekeepers. With the establishment of the sewing machine, the need for hand-stitching waned during the earlier part of the twentieth century, and interest in decorative needlecrafts took a tumble. In the last twenty years, however, people have once again become enthusiastic about needlecrafts, and cross stitch is the most popular because, once mastered, anyone can do it.

Cross stitch is a versatile medium for stitching. It allows you to create unique designs with only a needle and thread. Working from an easy-to-follow chart, even novices can produce elegant pictures to grace their homes. The stitches grow quickly, and you can watch the work develop before your eyes. It is an incredibly satisfying experience and a thrill when you can turn to friends and say "I did that."

These pages bring together 30 beautiful designs that everyone will want to stitch. We have compiled a collection of designs ranging from the simple, quick and easy to more complicated, detailed designs that will challenge

even the most accomplished needle worker. The projects have a seasonal theme, with designs for spring, summer, autumn and winter. Each one comes with a chart and key, and for those that need making up, there are step-by-step instructions to guide you through. In the back of the book step-by-step instructions are given for the basic stitches used. If you are new to cross stitch, refer to these pages before you start. Instructions are also given for filling a card, decorating a pot and lacing a picture. Inspirational ideas for mounting your work will make you realize how effective cross stitch can be for so many different occasions and have you itching to start stitching!

Each symbol on the chart represents one stitch. Parts of the design may be outlined in back stitch, this is identified by the solid heavy lines around or through the symbols. The colour for the back stitch details is included in the instructions. The key tells you which colour strand of cotton to use for each area. Because different manufacturer's threads are not exact equivalents, we have simply given you the colours. Other stitches such as French knots are included in the instructions.

Finally, the stitch count gives you the finished size of your design: the first number is the height and the second the width.

BIRD BATH

Spring brings with it the first birds out looking for food. Along with the first signs of colour and new growth, the birds symbolize the beginnings of a new season.

MATERIALS

fabric: 28 hpi evenweave over two threads, 10 x 10 cm (4 x 4 in)
stranded cotton, as listed in key
needle
mount board (backing board)
scissors
fabric-marker pen
wadding (batting)
pins
thread
oval frame

1 Work the cross stitch using two strands of stranded cotton for the bird, birdbath and grass. Use one strand for the remainder of the cross stitch.

2 Using one strand, back stitch dark brown grey around the birdbath. Back stitch the beak and legs of the black bird with two strands of dark lemon. Use two strands of dark lemon wrapped once around the needle for the eye. Use two strands of white wrapped twice around the needle for French knots on the grass, to represent daisies.

3 Lace the work and mount in an oval frame.

KEY

△	mid grey
▲	dusky rose pink
⊥	rose pink
◁	turquoise
▶	yellow leaf green
●	pearl grey
○	light mocha
✕	deep mocha
+	dusky yellow
■	sunshine yellow
☐	black

back stitch:
dark brown grey
dark lemon

French knot: white

stitch count 31 x 61

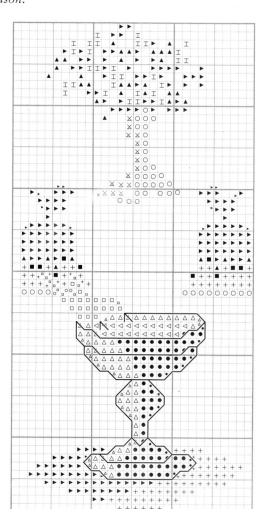

POSY OF PANSIES

Giving a card to someone you love reminds them how much you care.
Make this floral posy as a special gift.

MATERIALS

fabric: 14 hpi aida, 13 x 16 cm
(5 x 6¼ in)
stranded cotton, as listed in key
needle
scissors
glue
wadding (batting)
fabric-marker pen
card with aperture (opening)

KEY

⊐ light lemon

— lemon

| green grey

|| mid blue violet

+ violet

⋈ beige

back stitch:
violet
lemon
hunter green

stitch count 41 x 61

1 Work the cross stitch, beginning at the centre of the design. Use two strands of stranded cotton for all the cross stitch.

2 Once all the cross stitch is complete, use one strand of stranded cotton to create outlines in back stitch. Outline the pansies, bow, doily and "faces" of pansies in violet; the pansy detail in lemon and the leaf and stem outlines in hunter green.

3 Neatly finish the work and mount in a greetings card.

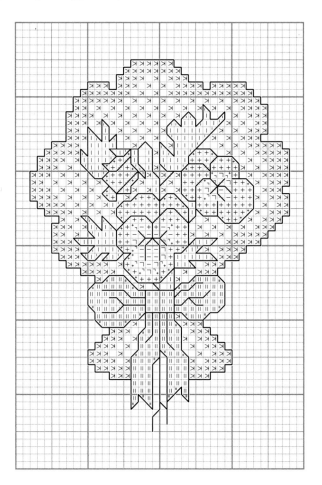

BLOSSOM TREE

*Pale pinks and pastel greens bring the blossom tree to life. Delicate shades of
emerging colour create a profusion of beauty unique to this time of year.*

MATERIALS

*fabric: 28 hpi evenweave over
two threads, 10 x 10 cm (4 x 4 in)
stranded cotton, as listed in key
needle
scissors
fabric-marker pen
crystal (glass) frame*

KEY

☒	light beige brown
●	medium beige brown
0	very light cranberry
↖	light baby pink
+	cranberry
◁	light pine green
▶	very light avocado green

stitch count 31 x 31

1 Work the cross stitch using two
strands throughout.

2 Neatly complete the work. Using
the aperture (opening) of the
frame as a guide for size, mark and
cut the design to fit the frame.

FIRST SNOWDROPS

Emerging through the new-fallen snow, the snowdrop peeks out its delicate head,
bringing with it a promise of new life and rich potential for the new year.

MATERIALS

fabric: 28 hpi evenweave over two
threads, 11 x 13 cm (4½ x 5 in)
stranded cotton, as listed in key
needle
fabric-marker pen
tape measure
scissors
wadding (batting)
oval pot

1 Work the cross stitch using two
strands throughout.

2 Back stitch the detail marked on
the chart using one strand of
mid parrot green.

3 Neatly finish the work and place
in an oval pot.

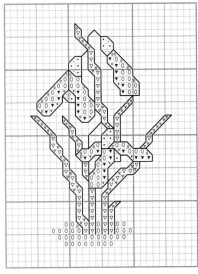

KEY

•	deep yellow green
▽	pale yellow green
▼	cream
○	white

back stitch:
mid parrot green

stitch count 31 x 41

PIG POT

*People love pigs, especially cheeky pigs. Surprise your friends by stitching them
this charming pot. It will make their day!*

MATERIALS

*fabric: 18 hpi aida, 10 x 10 cm
(4 x 4 in)
stranded cotton, as listed in key
needle
fabric-marker pen
scissors
wadding (batting)
6 cm (2¼ in) pot*

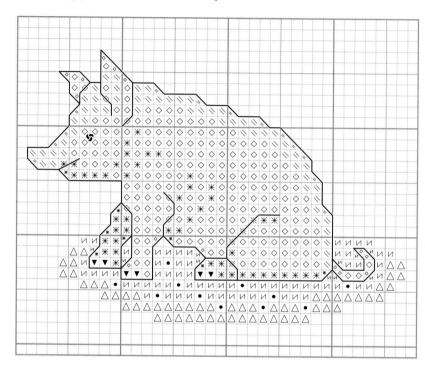

1 Starting from the centre of the
design, work the cross stitch
using two strands for cross stitch and
one for all back stitch. Use one
strand of grey twisted twice around
the needle for a French knot for the
pig's eye.

2 When the work is complete
check over your work for marks.
If it is grubby you can rinse the
stitching in warm soapy water to
remove any marks.

3 Allow it to dry flat and press
lightly on to a towel so that you
don't flatten the stitches.

4 Neatly finish the work and
mount it in a round pot.

KEY

✳	dark pink
▼	grey
•	white
╲	light pink
И	dark green
◇	mid pink
△	light green

back stitch:
grey

French knot:
grey

stitch count 36 x 25

SWAN PURSE

*Keep your pennies safe in this useful purse. Easy to stitch and
simple to make, it's a design anyone could try successfully.*

MATERIALS

*fabric: 14 hpi aida, 15 x 15 cm
(6 x 6 in)
stranded cotton, as listed in key
needles
scissors
pins
tape measure
backing fabric
thread
10 cm (4 in) zip (zipper)*

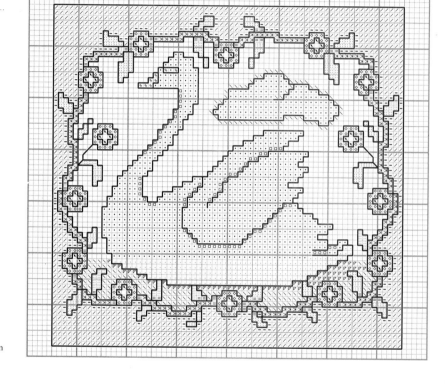

KEY

•	white
╲	black
□	pearl grey
—	dark navy
╱	navy blue
═	dark grass green
∴	bright green
↗	light green
◇	clover pink
⬚	lemon yellow
▽	mid sky blue
╲	light sky blue

back stitch:
black

stitch count 62 x 70

MAKING-UP INSTRUCTIONS

1 Work your cross stitch in two strands, back stitch in one. Take the piece with the design stitched on it and a piece of backing fabric the same size. With right sides together stitch 1 cm (½ in) at either end of the top edge.

2 Insert the zip (zipper). With right sides facing you place the zip behind the fabric. Tack (baste) and stitch the zip to the edge of the backing fabric. Then tack and stitch the front piece to the zip.

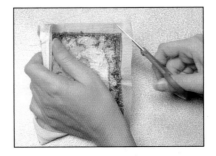

3 Open the zip slightly. Put right sides of the fabric together and stitch around the three open sides. Clip the corners. Unzip the purse and turn it to the right side.

BIRD BOOKMARK

You'll never lose your page again once you've made this decorative bookmark.
The appearance of the blue tit (blue bird) tapping away at a milk bottle is
a sure sign that spring is really here.

MATERIALS

fabric: bookmark, 18 hpi aida
8 x 18 cm (3¼ x 7 in)
stranded cotton, as listed in key
needles
scissors
felt
ruler
fabric-marker pen
pins
thread

KEY

•	flesh
⌐	black
ı	white
+	deep grey
•ı•	mid grey
÷	periwinkle blue
⊠	mid royal blue
⊠	pale yellow
0	pale green

back stitch:
black
deep grey

stitch count 31 x 101

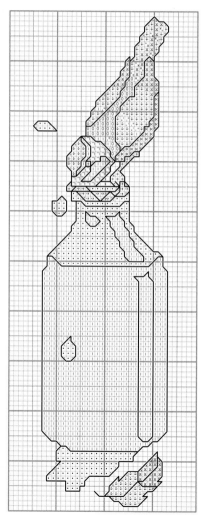

1 Work the cross stitch using one strand throughout.

2 Add back stitch details in one strand of black for the black facial markings, and deep grey for all other outlines marked on the chart.

3 Neatly finish the work. Cut a piece of backing felt slightly smaller than the bookmark. Pin the felt to the back of your work and, using a small stitch, oversew (slip stitch) the felt. Take care that the stitches don't show on the right side.

BABY FAWN

With the spring comes the new – new plants, new flowers and new animals. The fragile fawn, just born and finding its feet, evokes wonderful memories of the season of birth.

MATERIALS

fabric: 28 hpi evenweave over two threads, 12.5 x 12.5 cm (4¾ x 4¾ in)
stranded cotton, as listed in key
needle
fabric-marker pen
scissors
wadding (batting)
round pot

1 Work the cross stitch using two strands for the deer and also for the half cross stitch on the foreground scenery. Cross stitch the background foliage using one strand.

2 Back stitch the details marked on the chart using one strand in the following colours: deep beige for facial features; deep brown for outlining the deer; leaf green for the foliage and mid leaf green for the foreground greenery. Use one strand of white twisted twice around the needle for French knots for the eyes.

3 Neatly finish off the work and mount in the round pot.

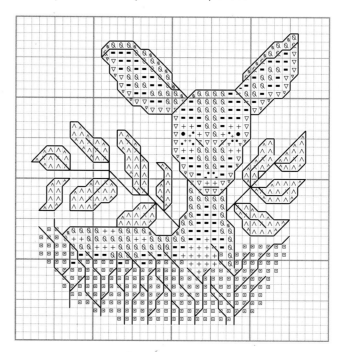

KEY

▽	light beige brown
◨	mid beige brown
■	very light beige brown
◼	green grey
●	black
∧	light yellow green
+	white

back stitch:
deep beige
deep brown
leaf green
mid leaf green

French knot: white

stitch count 41 x 41

OAK TREE HANGING

The mighty oak is a symbol of constancy – strong and eternal.
Create a beautiful hanging using this powerful subject.

MATERIALS

fabric: 28 hpi evenweave over two
threads, 19 x 19 cm (7½ x 7½ in)
needles
19 cm (7½ in) square medium
iron
iron-on interfacing
felt: 4 pieces each 7.5 x 2.5 cm
(3 x 1 in)
thread
felt
scissors
pencil
2 sticks each 20 cm (8 in) long
cord
2 tassels

KEY

■ dark green

⊞ mid green

+ light brown

▼ mid brown

• light green

back stitch:
grey
very dark green

stitch count
81 x 78

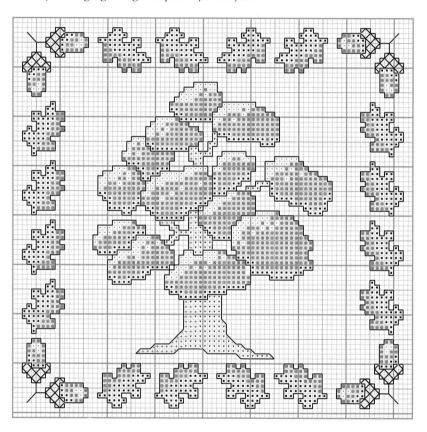

MAKING-UP INSTRUCTIONS

1 After working all cross stitch in two strands and all back stitch in one, iron interfacing to the wrong side of the embroidered piece. Fold small pieces of felt in half along the width. Tack (baste) them in position on the front piece.

2 With right sides of the large piece of felt and the evenweave together, stitch around three sides enclosing the small pieces of felt on the top and bottom edges, about 2 cm (¾ in) from corners.

3 Turn right side out and press. Slip stitch together the opening and insert sticks through the felt loops. Add a piece of cord with a tassel tied to each end across the top of the picture.

SUMMER GARLAND

This charming garland design will suit even a novice stitcher.
Whole cross stitch with back stitch detail make up this elegant
and simple design.

fabric: 28 hpi evenweave over
two threads, 15 x 12 cm (6 x 4½ in)
stranded cotton, as listed in key
needle
fabric-marker pen
scissors
wadding (batting)
crystal (glass) pot

1 Work the cross stitch using two
strands throughout.

2 Back stitch the detail, using one
strand, in the following colours:
grass green for stems on bottom half
of design; dark rose pink for centres
of pink flowers; sage green for stems
on top half of chart; dark purple for
detail on purple pansy and charcoal
for detail on violas.

3 Neatly finish the design and
mount in a crystal (glass) pot.

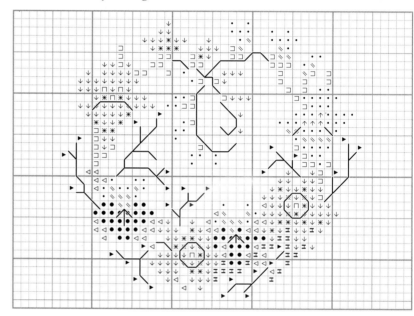

KEY

•	pale mauve	⊐	bright green
╲	mid mauve	I	pale sage green
↑	deep mauve	◁	deep khaki
↓	pale blush	▶	pale pink
✳	medium blush	●	buttermilk
⊓	very deep blush		

back stitch:
grass green
dark rose pink
sage green
dark purple
charcoal

stitch count 51 x 41

SUMMER ROSES HAT BAND

Add a touch of elegance to your summer hat by adding a decorative floral border.
Repeat this single rose design and you'll be the belle of the garden party.

MATERIALS

fabric: 14 hpi aida band, measure
around the hat, plus 10 cm (4 in)
stranded cotton, as listed in key
needles
pins
tape measure
scissors
thread
hat

1 Work the cross stitch using two
strands throughout.

2 Work the back stitch detail,
using one strand, in the following colours: dark pink around the
rose and dark green for the leaves.

KEY

• light pink

O mid pink

● dark pink

✕ dark green

✳ light green

back stitch:
dark pink
dark green

stitch count 61 x 31
(per repeat)

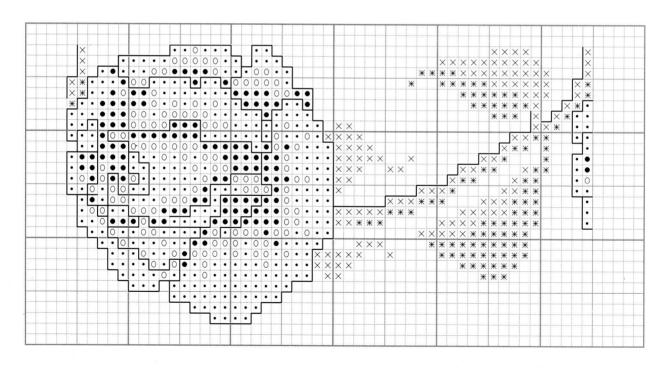

MAKING-UP INSTRUCTIONS

1 Measure the circumference of your hat and then divide the total measurement by two to get the centrepoint for the design. Using this measurement, mark the centre of the design on your band with a pin.

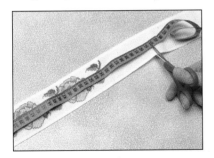

2 Work the design, stitching your first repeat from the centre point. Continue repeating the flower design to fit around the rim of the hat. Using the centre point as a mid measurement, cut the band to length allowing 5 cm (2 in) at either end for finishing.

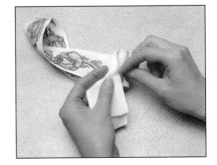

3 Place right sides together and stitch. Leave a 1 cm (½ in) seam allowance and press the seam flat. Turn the right way out and fit on to your hat with the seam at the back.

BUTTERFLY GIFT TAGS

*Flitting from bloom to bloom, the butterfly is a familiar sight during the summer
months. Wrap a summer gift and add a delicate tag to give a personal touch.*

MATERIALS

*fabric: 18 hpi aida, 16 x 9 cm
(6¼ x 3½ in)
stranded cotton, as listed in key
needle
wadding (batting)
gift tags with apertures (openings)
scissors
glue*

1 Work the cross stitch using two
strands throughout.

2 Back stitch the detail, using one
strand for each colour: dark
brown on the common butterfly and
black on the blue butterfly.

3 Neatly finish the work, and place
in a gift tag.

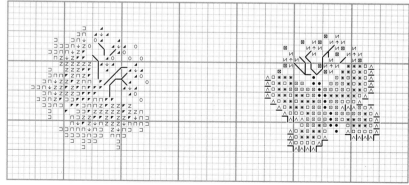

KEY

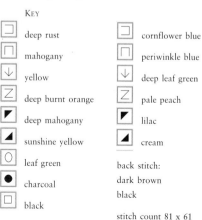

deep rust

mahogany

yellow

deep burnt orange

deep mahogany

sunshine yellow

leaf green

charcoal

black

cornflower blue

periwinkle blue

deep leaf green

pale peach

lilac

cream

back stitch:

dark brown

black

stitch count 81 x 61

LADYBIRD PAPERWEIGHT

You could use this paperweight to keep your kitchen notes and recipes tidy.
The ladybird is a versatile motif. Use the design to decorate a shelf border
and co-ordinate the room.

MATERIALS

fabric: 14 hpi aida, 13 x 13 cm

(5 x 5 in)
stranded cotton, as listed in key
needle
fabric-marker pen
scissors
8 cm (3 in) paperweight

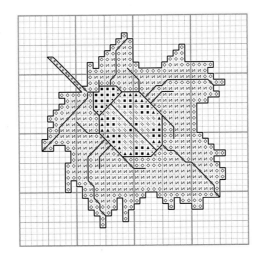

KEY

И	light green
◇	mid green
▲	light red
■	black
◣	dark red

back stitch:
dark brown

stitch count 33 x 34

1 First work your design using two strands for all cross stitch and one strand for all back stitch.

2 When complete, draw around the piece of felt supplied with the paperweight. Transfer the circle on to your design, centring the motif.

3 Cut neatly around the drawn line on the design.

4 Place the embroidery under the weight with the design facing into the paperweight and finish by placing the sticky felt on the base.

COLLECTOR'S ROSES

A collector's cabinet provides ideal storage for your personal trinkets.
Enhance it with this enchanting summer rose design for a truly superb display.

fabric: 28 hpi evenweave over
two threads, 15 x 15 cm (6 x 6 in)
stranded cotton, as listed in key
needles
yellow beads
cardboard
tape measure
scissors
wadding (batting)
glue
collector's cabinet

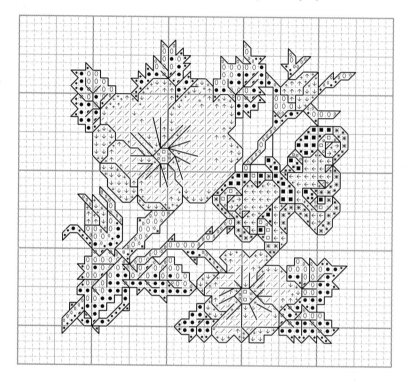

KEY

■	black
□	bright yellow
↓	rose pink
↑	pale rose pink
→	pale mauve pink
←	terracotta
✳	mid beige
○	bright green
●	deep fern green
╱	unstitched

back stitch: black

French knot: black

stitch count 51 x 51

1 Work the cross stitch using two strands throughout.

2 Back stitch the detail on the chart, using one strand of black. Stitch yellow beads for the ends of the stamen and stitch French knots in black on the end of the butterfly's antennae.

3 Finish the work. Cut the cardboard to the same size as the cabinet insert. Cut the wadding (batting) to the same size. Wrap the design over the card and wadding, and lace. Glue in the collector's cabinet.

COUNTRY FLOWERS SCISSORS CASE

Keep your embroidery scissors safe inside this easy-to-make scissors case.
Cornflowers and buttercups will make an heirloom case to keep the
blades clean and sharp forever.

MATERIALS

fabric: 2 pieces 28 hpi evenweave over
two threads, 12 x 15 cm (4½ x 6 in)
stranded cotton, as listed in key
needles
pins
scissors
lining fabric, 18 x 20 cm (7 x 8 in)
thread
lightweight iron-on interfacing
iron

KEY

+	lilac
∧	pale yellow green
И	pale yellow
\	dusky pink
/	dark cornflower blue
↓	mid leaf green
⊒	deep French navy

back stitch:
very dark cornflower
 blue
hunter green
dark mauve
deep canary

stitch count 31 x 51

1 Work the cross stitch using two
 strands throughout.

2 Back stitch detail, using one
 strand for each of the following
colours: very dark cornflower blue
for harebells and cornflower; hunter
green for stalks and leaves; dark
mauve for bow and deep canary for
cowslips and buttercups.

TIP

If you sew a piece of ribbon to
either end of the scissor case, you
can hang it around your neck and
never lose your scissors again.

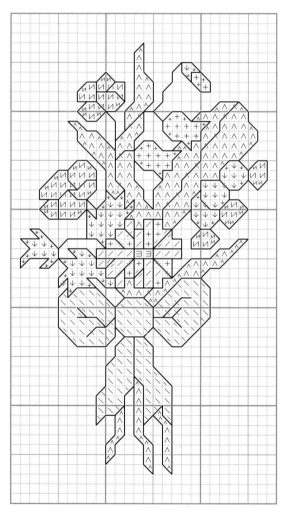

MAKING-UP INSTRUCTIONS

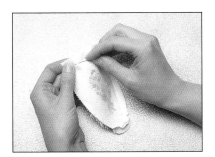

1 Cut two triangular pieces of lining and fabric; the top edge 7.5 cm (3 in) and the length 10 cm (4 in), with 2 cm (¾ in) extra on all sides. Work the design centrally on one piece of fabric. Iron interfacing on to the back of all four pieces. Pin one lining and backing piece right sides together and stitch along top edge, 1 cm (½ in) in. Do the same with remaining lining and front piece. Press flat with seams open.

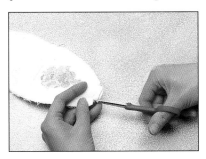

2 Pin the two pieces with right sides together and stitch around edge leaving a 4 cm (1½ in) gap at bottom of lining to allow for turning. Clip curves all along the edges.

3 Turn the work right side out and sew up the opening by hand with invisible stitches. To finish, tuck the lining inside the case.

LAVENDER BAG

Freshen up your wardrobe by hanging a sweet-smelling lavender bag.
The distinctive scent will remind you of long refreshing walks and summers past.

MATERIALS

fabric: 14 hpi aida, 15 x 16.5 cm
(6 x 6½ in)
stranded cotton, as listed in key
needles
pins
scissors
tape measure
45.5 cm (18 in) lavender ribbon,
3 mm (⅛ in) wide
thread
dried lavender

1 Work the cross stitch in two
strands throughout.

2 Back stitch the detail shown on
the chart, using one strand
of black.

KEY

✳	black
⊟	cream
⊟	deep green
●	sage green
○	pale sky blue
◁	pale periwinkle
▶	pearl grey

back stitch: black

stitch count 51 x 61

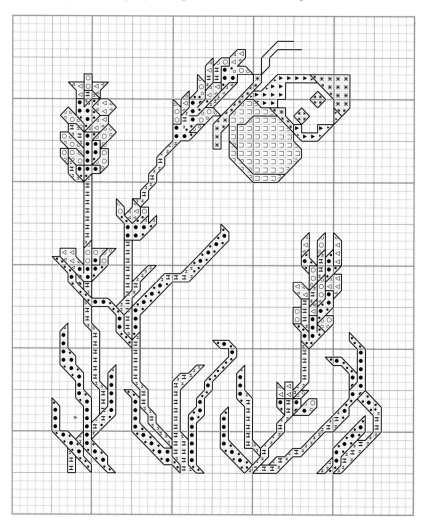

MAKING-UP INSTRUCTIONS

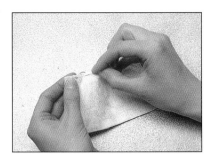

1 Fold under 1 cm (½ in) at the top of the work. Stitch to secure. With longer sides together, fold the work in half, right sides enclosed, and stitch along this seam leaving a 1 cm (½ in) edge.

2 Stitch a 1 cm (½ in) seam across the bottom of the bag. Turn to the right side and press. Taking a small pair of scissors, lightly snip vertically into the casing by the seam at the top of the bag at 1 cm (½ in) intervals. This is to form the ribbon casing.

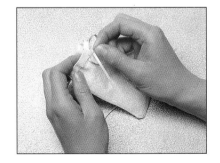

3 Thread the ribbon through the casing, using a large darning needle. Fill the bag with dried lavender and pull the ribbon to gather up the top. Tie in a bow to finish.

STRAWBERRY PAPERWEIGHT

*Lavish teas with fresh red strawberries epitomize all that is delicious
about lazy, hazy, warm summer days. This strawberry paperweight keeps
the memories fresh in your kitchen at all times.*

MATERIALS

*fabric: 14 hpi aida, 12.5 x 12.5 cm
(4¼ x 4¼ in)
stranded cotton, as listed in key
needle
scissors
fabric-marker pen
paperweight*

1 Work the cross stitch using three strands throughout.

2 Back stitch the detail on the chart, using one strand for each of the following colours: deep garnet around the strawberries; dark green around the leaves and on stalks.

3 Use one strand of very light beige, wrapped 2–3 times around the needle, for random French knots on the strawberries for seeds.

4 Neatly finish off the work. Cut to size and place face up in the paperweight. Finish by placing the sticky felt on the base.

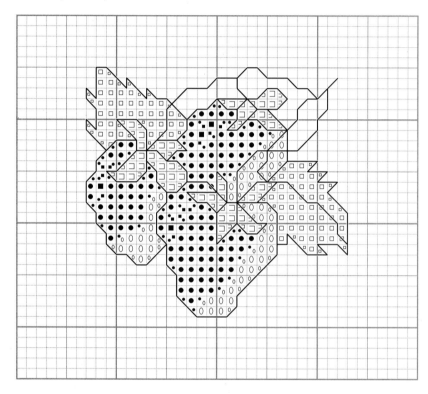

KEY

○	deep garnet	back stitch:
●	garnet	deep garnet
■	cream	dark green
⊐	mid grass green	French knot: very light beige
⊡	mid leaf green	

stitch count 41 x 41

BEES AND HONEY DISH TOWEL

Add a little decorative detail to your kitchen linen to grace your towel rail, by stitching this original yet simple hive design.

MATERIALS

*fabric: aida 14 hpi dish towel
stranded cotton, as listed in key
needle
scissors*

KEY

⊡	medium green
⊙	light green
⬤	pink
◸	golden brown
→	dark golden brown

back stitch:
dark green
dark pink
brown

stitch count 81 x 81 (per repeat)

1 Work the cross stitch using two strands throughout. Back stitch detail in the following colours: dark green for the leaf detail; dark pink for the flowers and brown for the hive (all two strands).

2 To stitch the work, start at the centre of the towel and stitch a hive with detail on either side.

3 Leave four holes before working your next repeat. Balance the design by working the same element on both sides of the centre.

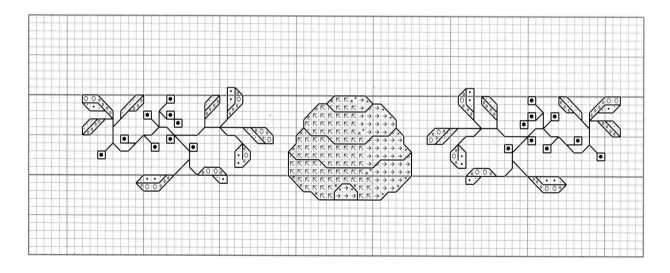

HALLOWE'EN PUMPKIN

*Fields of pumpkins and boughs full of red and green apples symbolize
this wonderful time of year, and make a perfect design for
a special Hallowe'en card.*

MATERIALS

*fabric: 28 hpi evenweave over two
threads, 14.5 x 12.5 cm (5½ x 4¾ in)
stranded cotton, as listed in key
needle
fabric-marker pen
scissors
wadding (batting)
card with aperture (opening)
glue*

KEY

✳	pink
•	black
I	light grey brown
+	dark grey brown
⊠	red
⊠	light green
∧	brown
И	dark gold
⋝	light gold
⋮	dark gold brown
●	dark green

back stitch:
black
brown
green
yellow
dark gold brown

stitch count 51 x 41

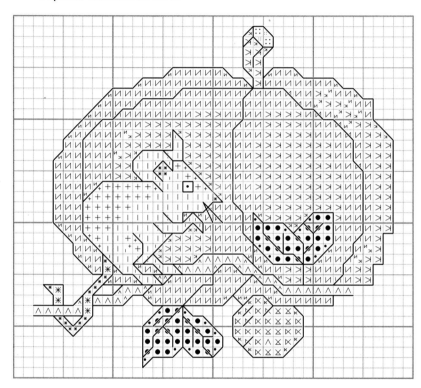

1 Work the cross stitch in two
strands throughout.

2 Back stitch the detail, using one
strand for each of the following
colours: black around the eye; brown
around the mouse and whiskers;
green around apple and leaf veins;
yellow for highlights on apple, and
dark gold brown around the stalk
and on the pumpkin.

3 Neatly finish off the design and
mount in the card.

AUTUMN LEAVES POT STAND

With its large leaves and fruit, the horse-chestnut makes a distinctive seasonal image. In an arrangement with oak leaves and acorns, it provides a perfect design for this pot stand.

MATERIALS

fabric: 28 hpi evenweave over two threads, 15 x 15 cm (6 x 6 in) stranded cotton, as listed in key needle tape measure fabric-marker pen scissors pot stand

1 Work the cross stitch in two strands throughout.

2 Back stitch the detail, using one strand for each of the following colours: very dark avocado green for oak leaves and very dark mocha brown for the remainder.

3 Neatly finish off the work. Cut to the same size as the aperture (opening) and place inside the pot stand. Secure with the backing card provided with the stand.

KEY

⊐ deep mustard

‖ mustard

+ mahogany

•⦙• pale mahogany

⦙ cream

∧ mid sienna

И pale sienna

◇ mid beige

∴ olive green

▶ deep beige green

back stitch:
very dark avocado green
very dark mocha brown

stitch count 51 x 51

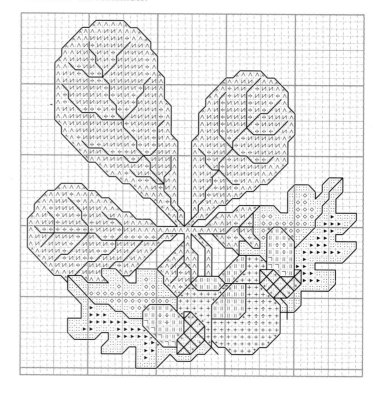

APPLE AND PEARS PLACE SETS

Cross stitch is so versatile, you can use it for almost anything. Creating a complete place setting can be satisfying, practical and extremely attractive – use the same chart for each, picking out either the pear or the apple for the napkin holder.

MATERIALS

fabric: ivory 11 hpi aida,
35 x 30 cm (14 x 12 in)
ivory 11 hpi waste canvas, approx
12 x 12 cm (4½ x 4½ in)
ivory 18 hpi aida, 7 x 7 cm (2¾ x 2¾ in)
stranded cotton, as listed in key
needles
napkin
napkin holder
scissors
fabric-marker pen
tape measure
iron-on interfacing
iron
cream cotton backing fabric
pins
thread

1 For the napkin, tack (baste) the waste canvas to a corner of the napkin and stitch the design, using three strands throughout. Dampen and remove the waste canvas and tacking (basting) stitches.

2 For the napkin holder, stitch either the pear or the apple using one strand throughout. Trim the aida to approx 5 x 5 cm (2 x 2 in) and iron under edges all round to make the finished piece approximately 4 x 4 cm (1½ x 1½ in) to fit napkin holder. Insert into holder.

3 For the placemat, position the design 4 cm (1½ in) up from the bottom edge of the fabric and 4 cm (1½ in) in from the left-hand edge. Use three strands throughout for the cross stitch.

4 Turn under the edges by 1 cm (½ in) all around, and iron flat. Take a piece of medium weight iron-on interfacing 33 x 30 cm (13 x 12 in) and iron on the reverse of the design, placing it between the turned edges.

5 Take a piece of cream-coloured cotton backing fabric measuring 35 x 30 cm (14 x 12 in), turn under a 1 cm (½ in) edge all around and press. Place on reverse of placemat with the turned edges sandwiched together, pin and oversew (slip stitch) the backing to the placemat.

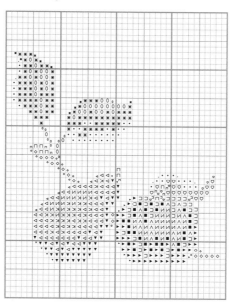

KEY

✳	mid pistachio green
•	dark pistachio green
⊅	light yellow beige
○	light pistachio green
▼	mid golden olive
◁	mid yellow beige
▶	mid avocado green
И	very light avocado green
■	light avocado green
∧	coral
⊐	dark coral
⊓	very dark beige grey
▽	very dark pistachio green
◇	deep beige grey

stitch count 41 x 51

BLACKBERRY CARD

*Do you remember autumn afternoons spent collecting delicious blackberries
to make jelly? Stitch this card in memory of those times.*

MATERIALS

*fabric: 18 hpi aida, 13 x 11 cm
(5 x 4½ in)
stranded cotton, as listed in key
needle
scissors
fabric-marker pen
wadding (batting)
card with aperture (opening)
glue*

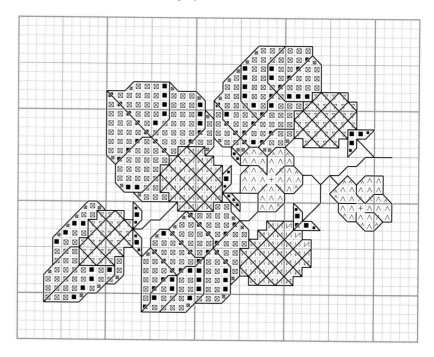

1 Work the blackberries and flowers using two strands of cross stitch. Use one strand for cross stitching the leaves.

2 Back stitch the detail, using one strand, in the following colours: very dark dusky rose for the flowers; dark antique violet for unripe blackberries; black for ripe blackberries and hunter green for the leaves.

3 Neatly finish off the work and mount in a greetings card.

KEY

▽ deep raspberry

∧ soft candy pink

Ͷ mid mauve

+ bright yellow

⊠ mid pine green

■ yellow green

back stitch:
very dark dusky rose
dark antique violet
black
hunter green

stitch count 51 x 41

NESTING SQUIRREL POT

Saving his store of nuts for the winter, the squirrel hoards and stockpiles.
This useful pot design celebrates his perennial task. Why not stitch some
for friends so they can hoard their trinkets inside?

MATERIALS

fabric: 18 hpi aida, 13 x 11 cm
(5 x 4½ in)
stranded cotton, as listed in key
needle
scissors
fabric-marker pen
wadding (batting)
round pot

1 Cross stitch all four leaves using one strand, and use two strands for the rest of the design.

2 Back stitch the detail using one strand of very dark mahogany throughout the design.

3 Neatly finish the work. Mount in a round pot.

KEY

✳	dark khaki green
O	mid mahogany
●	light khaki green
↑	very dark coral red
↓	very light brown
←	light tan
→	light mahogany
◁	white
▶	dark beige brown
Ͷ	black
☐	pearl grey
☐	light beige brown

back stitch:
very dark mahogany

stitch count 51 x 41

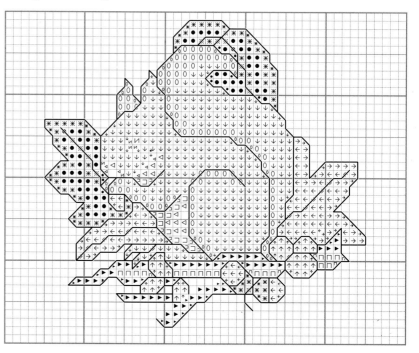

BIRD TABLE

It's not easy for birds in winter. The pickings are poor, but some kind people make their lives more pleasurable by stretching out the hand of generosity and leaving them titbits.

MATERIALS

fabric: 14 hpi aida, 16.5 x 18 cm
(6½ x 7 in)
stranded cotton, as listed in key
needles
scissors
tape measure
wadding (batting)
mount board (backing board)
pins
thread
frame

1 Work the cross stitch using two strands throughout. Use two strands of light brown for back stitching on branches and lemon for blackbird's legs and beak.

2 Back stitch remaining detail using one strand for each of the following colours: dark steel grey for chaffinch and blue tit (blue bird); Christmas red for nut bag; black for blackbird and footprints; very dark mocha brown for robin, bird table and bread. Use two strands for French knots in lemon for blackbird's eye and black for others.

3 Finish off your work, lace it and frame.

KEY

•	steel grey
⌐	black
I	Christmas red
—	light peach flesh
+	light tan
÷	lemon
⊠	very dark mocha brown
∧	light turquoise
И	very light brown
↓	pearl grey
□	light lemon
O	dark mahogany
⊠	light yellow beige

back stitch:

light brown

lemon

dark steel grey

Christmas red

black

very dark mocha brown

French knot: lemon, black

stitch count 61 x 71

POINSETTIA ORNAMENTS

Brighten up your Christmas tree with these imaginative, easy-to-stitch ornaments.

MATERIALS

fabric: 18 hpi aida, 12.5 x 12.5 cm
(5 x 5 in)
stranded cotton, as listed in key
needle
scissors
fabric-marker pen
thread
polystyrene ball
glue
gold braid
ribbon

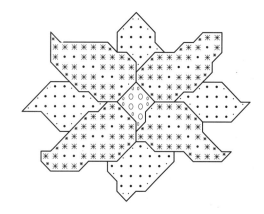

KEY

•	deep red
✳	Christmas red
O	yellow

back stitch:
black

stitch count 31 x 21

1 Work the cross stitch using two strands throughout. Back stitch around the outline, using one strand in black. Once the design has been worked, cut a circle from the fabric with the design in the centre. Run a gathering thread around the edge of the circle and pull it up around the polystyrene ball.

2 Attach a loop of braid to the top of the ball to make a hanging hook. Tie a bow from ribbon at the base of the braid.

3 Finish with a small circle of felt glued on to cover the gathering at the back of the ball.

MISTLETOE GIFT TAG

*When you give your Christmas presents, surprise the recipients with
dainty, hand-stitched tags.*

MATERIALS

*fabric: 18 hpi aida, 9 x 8 cm
(3½ x 3¼ in)
stranded cotton, as listed in key
needle
scissors
wadding (batting)
gift tag with aperture (opening)
fabric-marker pen
glue*

1 Work the cross stitch using one
strand throughout.

2 Back stitch the detail, using one
strand, in the following colours:
mid olive green for the left leaf and
deep olive green for the right leaf.

3 Neatly finish off the work and
mount within a gift tag, following the instructions on page 61.

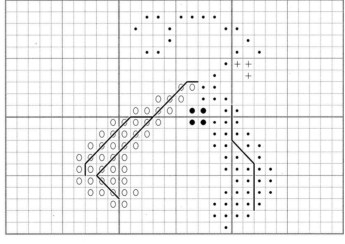

KEY

back stitch:
mid olive green
deep olive green

stitch count 31 x 21

•	deep olive green
O	mid olive green
●	cream
+	pearl

SPIDER IN WEB CARD

On cold, frosty mornings when the sparkling frost transforms the leaves and grass, the spider's web gleams like diamonds.

MATERIALS

*fabric: 14 hpi aida, 10 x 15 cm
(4 x 6 in)
needle
stranded cotton, as listed in key
wadding (batting)
glue
fabric-marker pen
scissors
card with aperture (opening)*

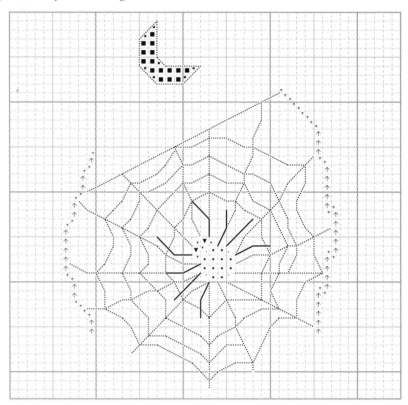

1 Starting from the centre of the design, work your motif using two strands for cross stitch, two strands of light grey for back stitch on legs and one strand of Kreinik silver for back stitch of the web. Use one strand for French knots in light grey for the eyes.

2 When the work is complete, check over it for marks. If it is grubby you can rinse the stitching in warm soapy water to clean.

3 Allow it to dry flat and press lightly on to a towel so that you don't flatten the stitches.

4 Neatly finish your work and mount in a greetings card.

KEY

•	light grey
▼	dark grey
↑	green
■	cream

back stitch:
light grey
Kreinik silver cord
French knot:
light grey

stitch count 32 x 42

Cyclamen Card

There is not much evidence of flowers during the winter months,
yet in households across the land the cyclamen blooms eternal.

MATERIALS

fabric: 18 hpi aida, 10 x 13 cm
(4 x 5 in)
stranded cotton, as listed in key
needle
scissors
fabric-marker pen
wadding (batting)
card with aperture (opening)
glue

1 Work the cross stitch using two
strands throughout.

2 Back stitch the detail, using one
strand, for each of the following
colours: dark cranberry around the
flowers and dark blue-green around
the leaves and stems.

3 Neatly finish your work and
mount in a greetings card.

KEY

∧	mid blue-green
И	light blue-green
\	dark blue-green
/	mid cranberry
⋊	light cranberry
0	dark cranberry

back stitch:
dark cranberry
dark blue-green

stitch count 31 x 51

ROBIN NEEDLECASE

*Stuck for ideas for Christmas presents? If so, why not make this
practical yet attractive needlecase?*

MATERIALS

*fabric: 28 hpi evenweave over
two threads, 4 pieces of 11 x 10 cm
(4½ x 4 in)
needles
stranded cotton, as listed in key
scissors
pins
tape measure
interfacing
felt
thread*

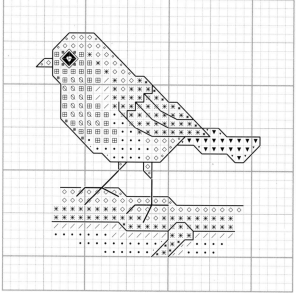

KEY

✳	mid brown
▼	dark brown
■	black
⊞	dark red
•	white
╱	grey
⊘	light red
◇	light brown

back stitch:
white
very dark brown
French knot:
white
stitch count
28 x 27

MAKING-UP INSTRUCTIONS

1 Cross stitch in two strands
and back stitch in one. Use one
strand for a French knot for the eye.
Iron interfacing to embroidered piece
and one other piece. With right sides
together, stitch two pieces of evenweave (one with interfacing) along
two long edges and one short edge.
Repeat with the other two pieces.

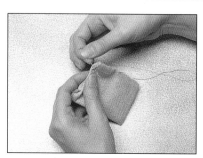

2 Turn both pieces right side out
and press.

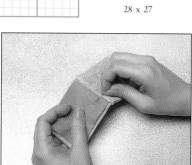

3 Stitch open edge together by
hand. Place these two rectangles
together, with felt between and stitch
through the three layers by hand.

CHRISTMAS TREE DECORATION

A simple flexihoop (embroidery frame) makes a super Christmas tree decoration. Stitch this tree to hang on yours. It's a project which can be attempted by the novice stitcher.

MATERIALS

*fabric: 28 hpi evenweave over
two threads, 11 x 13 cm (4½ x 5 in)
stranded cotton, as listed in key
needle
scissors
flexihoop (embroidery frame)
6.5 x 9 cm (2½ x 3½ in)
mount board (backing board)
wadding (batting)
pins
felt for backing
11 x 13 cm (4½ x 5 in)
thread*

1 Work the cross stitch using two strands throughout.

2 Back stitch the outline as marked on the chart with one strand of red stranded cotton.

3 Finish the work and place the design in the flexihoop (embroidery frame). Cut the fabric to within 2.5 cm (1 in) of the hoop and sew running stitches around the edge. Pull up the gathers and lace across the back (see page 63). Cut the felt to the same size and stitch the felt to the fabric.

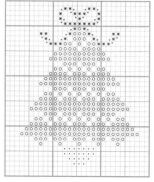

KEY

✳	red
•	brown
☐	green

back stitch:
red

stitch count 31 x 41

CROSS STITCH

This easy-to-make stitch is used as the basic stitch for all the projects in this book. With a crossing motion, take the thread across the weave into all four corners. You can use cross stitch to create the most beautiful and enduring needlework projects.

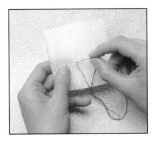

1 Bring your needle up at the bottom corner of a stitch. Take it down into the opposite top corner to form a half cross.

2 Bring it up in the adjacent bottom hole and finish the stitch by taking it down into the opposite top hole.

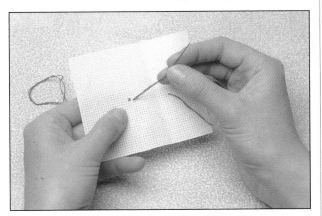

3 Repeat steps 1 and 2 for a row of stitches.

CONTINUOUS CROSS STITCH

If you're working large areas of a single colour, you may find it more efficient to use a continuous cross stitch. Work a strip of diagonal stitches, turn your needle and come back over the stitches, working the diagonal in the opposite direction.

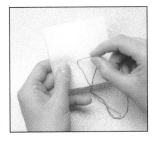

1 Bring your needle up through the fabric at the bottom corner of a stitch. Take it down in the opposite top corner.

2 Repeat this with the next stitch and the following ones, forming a row of half cross stitches.

3 When you have completed your row, turn the needle around and complete the stitches, forming the completing row across the first row.

FRENCH KNOTS

Texture and dimension can be given to your work by using French knots. The knot is a traditional embroidery stitch which complements cross-stitch designs beautifully.

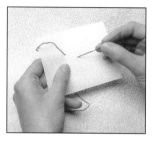

1 Bring the needle up through the fabric where you want the stitch to appear.

2 Make a small stitch and as you bring the needle back through the fabric wrap the thread twice around the needle close to the fabric.

3 Pull the needle through these threads, fixing the stitch by taking the needle back through the same hole where you started the stitch.

BACK STITCH

To add detail and definition to your work, back stitch is often used. It is a dense, straight stitch which creates a solid outline around a design.

1 Bring needle up one stitch length ahead of where you wish to begin. Drop it into the previous hole, bringing it up again two stitch lengths ahead.

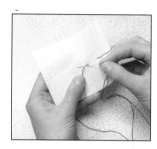

2 Repeat this step, taking the needle back one stitch length and bringing it back up two stitch lengths ahead.

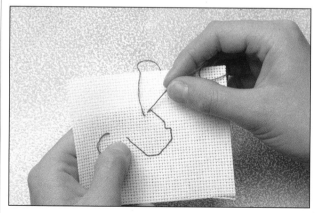

3 Should you wish to turn a corner, bring the needle up into the opposite corner, two stitch lengths ahead and continue stitching as above.

FILLING A CARD

There is a variety of ways to mount your work. One of the easiest and most useful is in a card. Cards with apertures (openings) are readily available from craft and needlework shops.

1 Place some wadding (batting) inside the wrong side of the aperture (opening). Draw around it with a marker pen.

2 Cut the wadding to the same size as the aperture on your card.

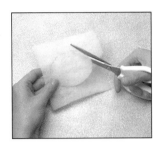

3 Cut down your embroidery to fit the middle section of the card.

4 Centre the design in the card, face down, so that the design can be seen through the aperture.

5 Place the wadding behind the aperture so that it fills the space and adds bulk behind the design.

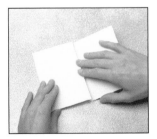

6 Stick the back section of the card to the middle with glue, adjusting the design to fit neatly as you do so.

DECORATING A POT

Pots with hand-stitched tops recall more gracious times when a lady's boudoir contained several powder bowls and trinket boxes. These elegant pots make superb gifts for friends to keep and treasure for ever.

1 Draw around the pot lid on to the wrong side of the embroidery, centring the design in the middle of the pot lid. Cut around this line, to give a circular or oval shape with your design in the middle.

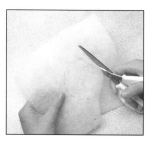

2 Draw around the wadding (batting) in the same way. Cut the wadding to the same size as the design.

3 Place the embroidery and the wadding face down in the lid. Secure your design by fixing with the metal disc.

LACING A PICTURE

Many people mount their work flat and glue it to a mount board (backing board) before framing. This is not a good idea. If you flatten your stitching you will not show its full beauty, and some glues will ruin your work. Use this method instead.

1 Cut some mount board (backing board) to size. Cut a piece of wadding (batting) smaller than the board. Ensure the embroidery is larger than both pieces.

2 Lay the embroidery face down, with the wadding and the board on top. Wrap the finished embroidery over the board and carefully pin it to the board's edges.

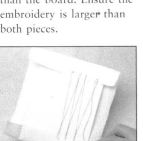

3 By stitching from the middle to the outer edge, start lacing towards the top of the work.

4 Repeat from the middle to the bottom, pulling the thread taut as you move along the edge.

5 Starting from the middle on the adjacent sides, lace the remaining two sides.

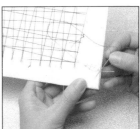

6 Turn in the corners and oversew (slip stitch) them together. Neaten by cutting off the stray threads.

 # INDEX

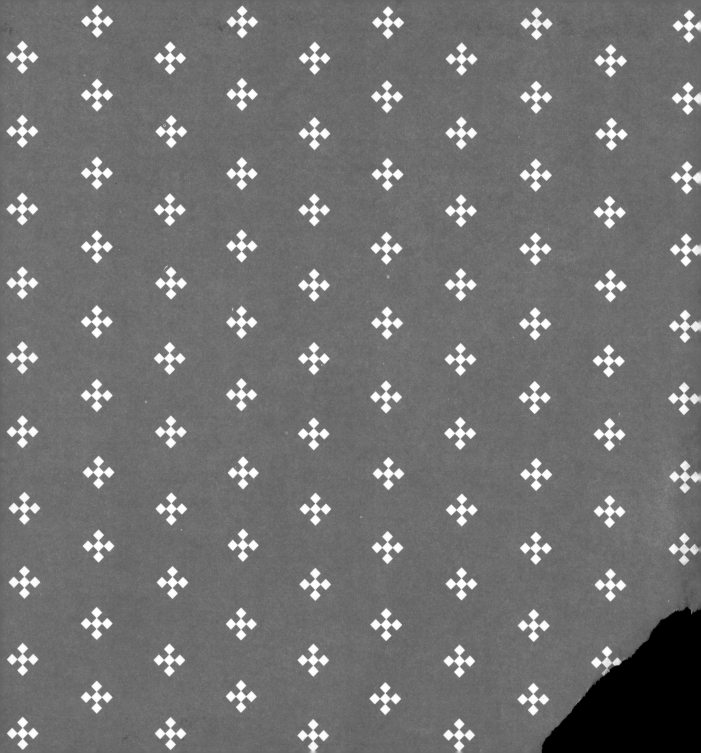